SRI DURGA DEVI TEMPLE
OF
TELLIPPALAI

Preface

Sri Durgadevi Temple of Tellippalai, in the North of Jaffna Peninsula, has become one of the most popular places of Saiva worship in the last few years. It is no more the temple which catered to the religious aspirations of the god fearing, of its surroundings alone. It has acquired a prominent place in the hearts of all Saivites living throughout the length and breadth of Sri Lanka. It has risen from the place of a village temple to that of a national one within a short period.

Erlalai M. Kandiah presents a monograph on this famous temple. The early history of this temple is shrouded in mystery. However, the author has attempted to cull out facts from the traditions prevalent in the area about the temple and presented a connected narrative for the reader. He is on firmer ground as far as the modern period is concerned. The narrative of the modern period is fairly extensive and gives details of the many attempts made by devotees of Durga to make her environs a national movement of veneration. The author has inscribed these devotees involved in the *Sivadharma* for posterity.

The author has given a detailed account of the present temple complex for the benefit of those who are not well familiar with its environs. Being a person well versed in the Agamic descriptions of temple structures the author has been careful in describing all the architectural and sculptural works seen in the temple. No one will need the help of a guide if he is aware of the descriptions given by the author in this monograph.

The author also clearly informs the activities springing from this holy temple and shows the importance it plays in the life of the Saivites. One cannot repute his parallel to the famous Chola temples of the Medieval times in this aspect.

The author has crowned his monograph with an essay on the place of Durga worship among Saivites and an explanation of it. He has to his credit publications on Saiva Rituvals and Saiva Siddhanta which clearly demonstrate his ability in this field.

The worship of God as father or mother or as both has been prevalent among the ancients according to their social set up. There are references to the worship of mother goddess in Tamil literature from the time of the Ancient Lyrical Poetry. Symbolism has added many forms to her and she is now worshipped in many names. Further local duties too have coalesed with her. Simple rituvals have been made complex with the march of time. Whatever the form she has been given she remains the fount of solace to those who need it and ask for it.

I am very happy to give this preface to a publication on Sri Durgadevi Temple with which my association had been very intimate and long. Members of my family have been closely associated with the growth of this temple and that of the Mavidda-puram temple for a long time. I was also associated with the activities undertaken by the Devasthanam of the temple in connection with conferences, publications and renual ceremonies. The Durga Devasthanam has also contributed a large sum of money to the University of Jaffna, for the endowment of a Chair in Saiva Siddhartham. I pass the Devasthanam daily on my way to office & back from my residence at Tellippalai. I am therefore, fully aware of the role played by this temple in relegious and social spheres.

Vidvan M. Kandiah was a student of mine at the University & is closely associated with the Durga Devasthanam. I wish to congratulate Vidvan Kandiah on bringing out this valuable monograph and pray to Goddess Durga to shower her grace on him so that he may bring out many more publications of this nature.

(Professor S. Vithiananthan)
Vice-Chancellor

Foreword

Many devotees in Sri Lanka and abroad have asked for a publication in English about Sri Durgadevi Temple of Tellippalai. This felt need has been very ably fulfilled by Erlalai M. Kandiah who is a very old devotee of this temple. As one who is closely associated with temple activities he has compressed within three chapters of this monograph most of the valuable information about this shrine.

I am very grateful to the Vice-Chancellor of the University of Jaffna, Prof. S. Vithiananthan, Professor of Hindu Civilization, Prof. K. Kailasanatha Kurukkal and the Registrar Mr. V.N. Sivarajah for their encouragement and very valuable contribution tothis publication.

May the blessings of Sri Durgadevi be bestowed on all.

President
Sri Durgadevi Temple Devasthanam

Select Opinion

Hindu temples are monuments which have often served to recount the glories of the Society of the people living around them. These temples, as a rule, conform to the agamic regulations in all their details. They are constructed according to the rules laid down in these text's, they also adhere to the pattern of religious activities prescrived therein. However, deriations were bound to occur. It is nothing but natural that these institutions often came under the influence of the environments of the locality in which they were situated. The temples had thus to assimilate the local traditions and thereby evolve new patterns, without much deriation from the fundamentals, as a result of this integration of local tradition, they possess a wealth of information and when called upon they can very well recount the glories of the culture of the people who live around them and worship in them for generations.

Sri Kandiah in this respect has made a pioneer attempt to present in this monograph a brief account of the history of a temple of his choice. He has, in this study of the Durga temple of Tellipalai, attempted in his own way to narrate the glories of the part of the Hindus of Sri Lanka. Indeed the glories depicted in this study of temple are those of the Hindus who have made a distinctive contribution to the advancement of Hindu Civilisation in Sri Lanka as well.

Similar studies of Hindu temples situated elsewhere in Sri Lanka should follow this exemplery attempt made by the author. When the results of all such studies are brought together, a connected History of Hindu Civilisation Sri Lanka could be systematically produced.

University of Juffna
31-10-1986.

Professor K. Kailasanatha Kurukkal
Head of the Department of
Hindu Civilization.

Contents

Bibliography

1. Thirumoolar Thirumantram

2. Rig Vedic Hymns—
   Durgaasooktam
   Devi Sooktam
   Sri Sooktam

3. Silappathikaaram

4. Aagama—Poorva Agama Kaarana

5. Tholkaapiyam

6. Thirumurukaatruppadai

7. Vyaagraasura Legend by
   Chariot Construction Souvenir 4.9.1978,

8. Maarkandeya Puraana

9. Saiva Siddhanta Mahasamayam
   Red Coral Jubilee Souvenir

10. Financial Reports published by the
    Board of Trustees.

Introduction

This book is a marvellous microcosm. Within three chapters the author has condensed three major themes namely

— the meaning of worship of Durga Goddess;

— the role of the Tellippalai Durga Temple; and

— the history of the temple.

The origin of Durga worship is traced to the saga of the Agamas and Vedas and the theological and philosophical aspects are dealt with clarity and depth of understanding in the first chapter. The word meaning of Durga is given as "the deity of fortress as she is difficult to approach". The manifold aspects of Goddess Durga are presented to the devotee based on important sources. This deity is :

— the manifestation of Siva in a sort of flower and fragrance relationship;

— the energy responsible for connecting the fruit of karma and the soul;

— the mother of the tender child Muruga or Skanda;

— the victorious over the evil demons;

— the embodiment of Saraswati, Luxmi and Gowri;

— the embodied form of :

—volition	—Iccha Sakthi
—conation	—Kriya Sakthi
—cognition	—Gnana Sakthi

— the unism of the three natures of Grace

Satvic

Thamas

Amidst the vast ocean of Goddess worship concepts from ages immemorial, related puranic legends and mythologies and iconographic presentations *the author identifies "the form installed in our temple at Tellippalai as saatvic*".

Having identified the icon the interpretation of the icon is given in the following words:

> "*Its facial expression is calmness*
> It has the bare minimum of four hands wielding the conch, the discus, the trident and the skull........ our deity here is born with the attributes belonging to both Vishnu and Siva. The conch and discus are of Vishnu and the trident and the skull are of Siva".

The significance of the four attributes are also given—

The Conch reveals sakti's attachment with Pranava which is expressed in the conch by its form and sound;

The discus signifies here being the wielder of power;

The trident mention that she is an embodied form of Icchaa, Kriya and Gnana, the volition, conation and cognition respectively.

The skull stands as a sign of her being even after everything is reduced to its final stage of perish and thereby it is she who causes the destruction on behalf of her Lord Siva.

The thesis is that "Totally all these amount to show that our deity is note other than Parasakthi and she is Durgaparameswari".

He has added that "the solemn calm and graceful lusture radiating from the face of this deity may increase an insatiable thirst for worship".

The second chapter deals with the structure and the layout of the temple:

- the architectonic aspects such as the symmetry, the architectural excellence, the artistic beauty and the sculptural embellishments;
- the systematic and efficient management of this temple;
- the function of the temple in society, the role this temple plays in raising the moral and religious perspectives of particularly the youth and the intensive impact of the temple on the saiva public;
- the manner in which the temple serves the poor and the rich, the learned and the unlearned, the begger and the affluent, the young and the old in regard to their varied spiritual and socio-religious needs.
- the ways in which "this temple generously allows a good part of its abundance to be channelled toward the propagation of Siva dharma within and without its bound in activities such as;
    - Fostering of cow ( )
    - Running an orphanage;
    - Conducting a centre for destitute women;
    - Having regular classes for disseminating religious knowledge;
    - Training Saiva Children and Youths in the chanting of devotional hymns;
    - Maintaining a centre for training temple priests;
    - Producing a feeding centre;
    - Contributing for flood relief; refugee relief, medical relief and educational needs.

The Thirupathy temple and the temples under Chola regime and this temple are held as examples for others to emulate.

Two major events and the commanding heights reached in each case are brought out well as "these two events have contributed much to the advancement of the religious and the cultural atmosphere of the temple.

"Of all the religious sessions held under the auspices of this temple, the red coral Jubilee of the Saiva Siddhanta Maha-samjam of Mylapoor voluntarily called to be held here was held supreme".

Significant in similar manner is the "Chandihoma" which is held as the greatest out of all the extensive special agamic rites conducted by this temple. The Chandihoma was headed by no less a person than Professor Dr. K. Kailasanatha Kurukkal, Professor of Hindu Civilization of the University of Jaffna, the author of several books and a living authority on Hinduism and Hindu rituals in particular.

The Third chapter is temple history in brief. The period covered is from about 1820 to the present day. Records are available only for the last three decades. The consecration in 1820 after its demolition by the Portugeese and the visit of the deity of the Maviddapuram temple in 1829 are historical land marks. In the case of some other temples such as the pre Vijayan temples some facts before the Portugeese destruction of places of worship are known. In the case of the Durga Devi Temple the pre Portugeese position has not been researched.

The significance of the unbroken traditional link between this temple and the famous Murugan Temple of Maviddapuram has been brought out in its religious, mythological and sociological dimensions. The link primarily is one of mother and tender child. The mother and child formed an alliance to defeat the twin asura forces. Lord Muruga visits annually on the last day of Navarathiri the temple of his mother. This festival is comparable to the Vel festival of Colombo. This festival promotes the social participation of all the villages extending from Maviddapuram to Tellippalai and recently from all parts of Jaffna. People flock in large numbers to witness the ritual drama of the Durga killing the Demon depicting the victory of Goodover Evil on Vijayadasami Day.

This chapter mentions in brief the personalities involved in the growth of this temple from the founder Kadirgamar to the present day Thangammah Appakutty, elected President of the Governing Trust in 1977. Sir Kandiah Vaithianathan the late Manager and Secretary of the restoration society of Thiruketheeswaram had laid the first stone in 1954 for the construction work over the foundation (Varikkal Naaddal).

The transfer of management from a family to a Board of Trustee is significant. In 1974 the Executive Committee celebrated the Silver Jubilee to mark the twenty fifth year of the services of Pundit Miss Thangammah Appakutty and awarded the honour "Durga Duranthiri" namely. The voluntary enshoulder of the monstrous work of restoration in honour of Goddess Durga. The development during the golden age enabled the temple to play its socio religious role quite effectively as was seen in the second chapter.

The tenor of the entire presentation is primarily devotional. The purpose of the author is to promote devotion with right understanding. The touch stone for all activities and social service, puranam recitals and philosophical discourses is the devotional atmosphere in which these are conducted and the reciprocal reinforcement of the religious atomosphere by these activities. The value of the book is enhanced by the fact that the scientific rigors of meticulous examination of source material and evidence and logical conclusions are maintained throughout while at the same time maintaining the fragrance of piety and devotion.

The author needs no introduction to those of the Saivite World and University circles. (A list of his publications is given in this book).

He is well known to the students and teachers of two of the subjects taught in Sri Lankan Schools and Universities namely Hinduism and Hindu Culture. The description of the subject in the University of Colombo is Hindu Culture. Mr. Kandiah's books are used as texts and for reference in these classes. He is accepted as an authority in the exposition of Saiva Siddhanta particularly in relating the basic tenets of philosophy to the religious texts and day to day life. He is an unostentious scholar who goes about in a Vetty and Shawl and is an illustrous example of a person of simple living and high thinking like the Mahatma.

This book is an indispensable work for a devout Hindu as well as scholars of "Saktism" namely the worshippers of the female energy in the background of the age old recognition of a dual practice in nature, purusha (male) and prakriti (female).

1

The Goddess Durga

The twin aspects of God as Siva and Sakti is a significant feature of saivism. How Siva is thus Sakti is. It is an accepted truth expounded in traditional saiva treatises. Though they are inferentially two yet there is no twoness to be found. Both of them are inseparably one even as the fire and heat, jewel and lustre, and flower and fragrance. Whatever aspect of divinity acclaimed to Siva is not without its share to Sakti. There is no Siva without Sakti and no Sakti without Siva, even when it is philosophically expounded that Sakti is the manifestation of Siva, the being of Siva in the manifestation, itself is implied to be.

The Sakti of Siva is named variously such as grace, power and energy. According to philosophical and theological threatises it is established that the Sakti, though it is formless like Siva becomes visible to seers and sages like Thirumooler in an innumerable forms of manifestation to be named variously as Gowri, Kaali, Umaa, Durgaa, Puvaneswari, Lakshmi, Saraswati, Rajesvari and Lalita all of them are one and the same in essence. Though they are sometimes distinguished as higher and lower deities for purposes of various functions attributed to them in the annuals of ceremonial settings all of them are same in substance.

Saivism in its long history has been admitting the worship of Siva with Sakti being an inseparable part of it. Yet to worship the different forms of Sakti as visualized by seers and sages also however has become inevitable and even then the concept of worship is not worshipping Sakti alone. The inseparableness of Sakti with Siva warrants that Siva is implied in the act of worshipping the Sakti forms. Saint Thirumoolar admonishes us that if you worship Sakti as it' sharing half with Siva you will have enlightenment and you will transcend the barrier of time—Thirumantiram 1069.

Goddess Durga is undoubtedly is one of the various forms'of Sakti revealed by itself to the seers and sages from long and long ago. The worship of Durga seems to be as old as the veda is. In the Rig veda there are hymns in the tytles of Durgasooktam, Devisooktam, and Srisooktham. The first two verses of the Durgasooktam, reveals the graceful form and functions of Durga as follows.

She appears in the form of yaagaagni—the sacred fire. She is all knower. She may destroy our enemies—the bad qualities personified in asuric forms. She may remove obstacles in our ways of spiritual as well as physical live. Let her take us ashore of the ocean of sin even as a boat does in the sea. She shines in fiery lustre of penance. She burns her asuric enemies with her fiery look. She is visible only to the eyes of pure wisdom and she is interested in joining the fruits of karma to the respective soul.

The second verse ends with a Salute saying 'Salute to her who unable us cross the ocean of birth.

'We also find a descriptive passage of verses sung on the Goddes Durga in the celebrated tamil literature Silappathikaaram of the 2nd century A.D. The contents of the passage is as follows.

She is clad in tiger skin and wears the elephant skin as her over coat. She stands on the black buffalo's head—a personification of ignorance. She is felt to be the inner secret of veda and shines like a tender shoot of enlightenment. She is adored even by the eminent gods. She is armed with a sword in hand. Having mounted a deer she went on war with the demon Mahisha and killed him. As an illuminating lamp she shines in the hearts of the Trinity. She wields the conch and the discuss-chakra, each on either hands Sometimes she appears mounting on a furious lion and the vedas pray and serve her as just half of Lord Siva.

The description in the above coincides with the illustration of

Sakti to be found in the Aagamas including the Thirumanthiram of Thirumoolar the authoritative works for Saivism. At the outset of the preceding passage we noted that the attire both the tiger skin and the elephant skin that are invariably ascribed to Siva are said to be her dress. The expositions that Sakti is responsible for connecting the fruit of karma with the soul and she is the sole activator in getting the soul ashore in the ocean of wordly ills and she is transcendent of the Trinity and she is inseparably one with Lord Siva are some facts expounded in Saivassiddhanta and this much is enough of to suggest that Durgadevi is none other than the paraasakti so characterised in saiva theology and philosophy.

The poorvakaarana Aagama provides rules for the installation of Goddess Durga in a chapter entirely devoted to it.

A chapter named as Thripurai chakram in the fourth book of Thirumanthiram illustrates in many verses the excellent beauty and the boundless grace of Thripurai one of the synonyms of Durga—vide: Thirumantiram Verses 1045—1074, edited by Kaasimadam Thirupananthal. The ephithet Thripurai means she who stands envoleping the three regions of the sun the moon and the Agni in the micro cosm and the macrrocosm. Thirumooler called her by various names and one of them is chandika which is also a synonym of Durga. Some aspects that Thirumoolar attributes to Thripurai keep pace with what we noticed in the vedic hymn in Sanskrit and the Silappathikaaram verses in Tamil.

Thirumooler says that she is the cause of cause. She is self manifested divine being. Where Lord is there she is. She is parai and paraaparai that shares Siva's form. She confers knowledge, enjoyment and liberation to the souls. She is an embodiment of Lakshmi Sarashwati and Gauri all together. She stands as the support for the tender vine of enlightenment Jnaana. He comes out with the true import of the Sakti as he sings that 'except her, I know not how to reach the city of Salvation'.

The vogue of erecting separate temple in honour of Durgadevi is traced to as early as the 9th century A.D. during which king vijayaalaya, the first of the later Cola dynasty is said to have effected a temple to Nisumba soothiri—the killer of the demon Nisumba—an epithet of Durga. But it does not mean that the worship of Durga started in the 9th century itself. The deity worship by the individuals is much more earlier than temple worship. The sculptors of lore had an special taste in engraphing the Durga forms. An sculpture of Durga of the 7th century found in Maamalla puram the famous city of Arts in south India is commended much for its expression of dreadfulness mingled with calmness.

The ancient kshetras include at least a shrine room for Durga within their bounds somewhere within and somewhere without the temple court yard, the inner praahaara or the circum ambulatory passage. In some towns Durga is installed as guardian deity and worshiped with due respect. In paddeecharam a reputed ancient Siva temple Durgadevi is installed in the front hall within the temple and honoured as the prominent deity of the temple. In Thiruvotiyoor Durga is installed in the northernside of the inner praahaara and worshiped in the name of Vaddapuri Amman with special rituals and festivals for fifteen days in a particular season every year. In Thiruvaaroor, the prominent Siva temple in the Tanchoor district Durga is installed outside the temple bounds in the name of Raaja Durgaa. In Vedaaranyam she is worshiped in the name of Kaadukaal or Kaadukilaal meaning the deity of the forest and it is held as a remnant of the habit of worshipping Durga as the principal deity of the desserts as laid down in Thol-kaappiam, the famous encyclopedia of Tamil Culture.

Durga is also worshiped in some other kshetras in her manifested form of Kaali. The deified forms of Kaali worshiped in the Thraupathi Amman temple at Kumpakonam and Chidamparam—Thillaikaali—are to be noted. Vide : Encyclopedia in Tamil, Madras edition Book 3, page 623.

That Durga was worshiped as an absolute deity form in the Saiva land has come down through both the Tamil canon and the Sanskrit Canon. In the canonical literatures she is known as Kottavai, Kotti, Kumari, and Kanni. In the later literatures she is mentioned as Imayakilavi and Kadumporkkanni, Kottavai-Kotta +Avvai—Victory+mother means—The goddess of victory.

Kumari and Kanni means the virgin. Imaya kilavi means the old deity of the mount Himaalaya. Kadumporkanni means the virgin going on furious war. Through the Sanskrit Canon she has been known as Thripura, Chandikaa, Chaamundi, Kaali and Durga, Durga means the deity of the fortress or she who is difficult to be approached. Chandikaa and Chaamundi means Victorious over the demons Chanda and Chaamunda by name. The common feature of all these names categorically point to Durga's Character of being ever victorious.

In Thirumurukaattuppadai, one of the canonical literatures in Tamil Lord Muruka is invoked as vetti velpor kottavai Siruval— the tender child of Durga known as victorious in the wars. The relationship of Durga with Muruka in the victory point of view is brought out well in the legend of Vyaaghraasura. The theme of the legend is that goddess Durga and Lord Muruka once formed an array against Vyaaghraasura who had the demon Mahisha as his alliant and in the ensuing war Durga killed Mahisha and Muruka Vyaaghraasura. Vide : the article Vyaaghraasura samhaaramoorthi in the Sovenier published on 4-9-78 by the executive committee of Durgadevi temple in commemoration of the chariot—construction. While dealing with the said legend the author of the article nicely brought to light the inner secret or the special significance of why the deity of Muruka from Maavidda-puram should visit the temple of Durgadevi on the occasion of Mahaanambu festival falls in the month of September year after year.

Of all the accounts of Durgadevi that has come down through Sanskrit Canon the one which is found in the Maarkandeya purana is celebrated. A chapter under the title of Devi Mahatmya in that purana contains 700 verse—form mantras known as the 'Saptasati' meaning, that which contains seven times hundred. The Saptasati is celebrated as the best for chanting and meditating on Durga and the other best use of it is to be obsarved when it is used in the elaborate sacrifice the chandihoma where in it adds much to the devotional flavour to be prevailed in the officiating priests and the worshippers participating in the homa ceremony. The saptasati is taken also as complimentery of the enchanting of the mystic formulae known as Navaakshasi which is said to be best to invoke the grace of Durga. The Navaakshari mentra renders as 'Aum-Aim-Hreem-Kleem-Chaamundaayai Vicce' meaning I know goddess chaamunda as the very form of the threefold, base-form mystic formulae Aim, Hreem and Kleem.

The saptasati is of immense value for so much as it expounds almost all the divine attributes and marvellous power of Durgadevi through simple legends easily appealing even to less cultured minds. The all embracing character and the all enveloping feature of manifestation of Durgaa are well defined in this portion of Maargandeya puraana especially in mantras 273-339 chap. 5. The axiomatic truth that the in and out of the entire soul cavity is exclusively filled in and moved by Durgadevi, the chandikaa is well portrayed in this section and thereby its excessive power of creating devotional atmosphere in the worshipers mind is enormous.

The bulk of different manifestations of Durgadevi seem to form a good part of Hind pantheon and this is mainly attributed to the saatvic raajasic and thaamasic nature of grace. She assumes in view of her gracious acts of liberating the good, protecting the passionate and destroying the vicious types of men respectively. (To destroy means the destruction of the bad qualities prevailing in one but not the soul). The most dreadful form of Durga is said to be Thamasic which may be seen to have several hands—eight, ten and even eighteen—wielding deadly weapons and also with terrible facial features such as knitting eye-brows and daring look. The form of Durga, the expression of which may be in a complex of dreadfullness mingled with calmness is said to be raajasic. The sculpture of 7th century at Maamallapuram refered to above can be suggested as an example to this type and that which is manifesting in a solemn beauty of calmness is called to be saatvic. It is also interesting to note that one and the same of these three forms may act differently on different worshiper as to get him gifted with what he deserves, provided his worship is just and proper.

Of the three forms mentioned above the one installed in our temple at Tellippalai is Saatvic. Its facial expression is calmness.

It has the bare minimum of four hands wielding the couch, the discuss the trident and the skull sometimes Sakti is identified with Vishnu and called Naaraayanee and always claimed to be one with Siva. It is remarkable that our deity here is born with the attributes belonging to both Vishnu and Siva. It is a form rarely met with in the bulk of deity forms of Sakti. The conch and discuss are of Vishnu and the rident and the skull are of Siva. The significance of these four attributes amounts to the special feature of our deity. The conch reveals Sakti's attachment with pranava which is expressed in the couch by it form and sound. The discuss signifies her being the wielder of power. The rident mentions that she is an embodied form of Icchaa Kriyaa and Jnaana the volition conation and cognition respectively. The skull stands as a sign of her being even after everything is reduced to its final stage of perish and thereby it is she who causes the destruction on behalf of her Lord Siva. Totally all these amount to show that our deity is non other than Paraasakty and she is Durga parameswari. The solemn calmness and graceful lustre radiating from the face of this deity may increase an insatiable thirst for worship on Her devotees.

2

The Temple

The temple of Durgadevi at Tellippalai is an object of more admiration than that of veneration in the era of its recent development. The rapid growth and the fast development of its edifices and the vivid colours and varigated beauties issuing forth from them create a good solemn taste and an indelible mark of imprint in the minds of pilgrims and devotees and as a whole the temple stands to be felt as a marvel.

In early thought of saivism any spot where in a marvel is enacted is undoubtedly a kshetra or a sacred spot or a field of divinity where in the process of an active power is already on the working. The kshetrahood or sacredness of the spot in reference i.e. the venue of the temple is to be traced to its very beginning that is said to be roughly three hundred years back. It is said that a saintly person known as Kathirkamer who himself is an ardent worshipper (upaasaka) of goddess Durga in a chakra—mystic diagram—form took shelter in an Iruppai—Bassia Longifolia—grove in ulukodai the exact site of the present temple. He installed the Durgadevi chakra at his worship at the foot of a tree there and rested worshiping the same.

Generally it is believed that the foot of a tree under which a saintly person could sit in contemplation retiring from his worldly alliances, becomes a sanctified spot and the tree itself is conceived as the haunt of divinity. It is quite evident from what we witness that the well flourished ancient kshetras include a sacred tree within their bounds and the tree too is venerated as Tala Vruksha the tree of the sacred spot and when an icon or anything equvalent to it installed in the same spot the sanctity of and divinity adds to it rises to an unimaginable level.

The natural affinity of divinity with some of the material things such as the tree the water spread, the ant hill and the mountain peaks claimed in the Bsihatsamhita and the Bhavishya puraana, the famous Hindu scriptures can be suggested as an scriptural evidence to this fact. So it is not far, from truth if we account the quick and steady development and the marvellous features of this temple to the contact with the particular Bassia Longifolia tree through saint Kathirkaamer. It is also to be noted that four of the same kind of trees are still found in the temple premises.

The awe inspiring sight of the depth and vast spacious dimension of the temple tankattracting the on comer with a long row of sculptural sacred pots set with the traditional mango leaves and the coconuts, on all the four sides the small but well looking edifices in the miniature form of shrine rooms with pretty domes in the four corners, the glittering long steps symmetrically laid with spotless white stones and the well painted and fashionably shaped dome (vimaana) over the shrine hall meant for the deity of Durgadevi's residence when the deity visits the tank for the festival of water—cutting ceremony, the admirably large and lofty size of the chariot stand, the all enveloping excellence of artistic beauty manifesting in the rows of carvings of the massive chariot, the imposing height along with the architectural excellence and the sculptural embellishment of the majestic raaja gopuram depicting the graceful functions of gods illustrated in the extent saiva puraanas, the solemn beauty of the niches enshrined with Dvaaraganapathi, Dvaarasubrahmaniya, the Sanganithi and Padumanithi in the front wall to be found on either side of the raaja gopuram and interposed with fashionable edifices are some of the salient features striking the devotional minds and directing them straight to the darson of Durgadevi enshrined in the sanctorum manifesting in boundless grace.

The cleanliness of the various halls, shrines and the first praahaara—the circum ambulatory passage of the inner temple—is maintained with meticulous care. The vimaana—the single tiered dome over the sanctum sanctorum and the projected shrine room of the mahaamandapam—the court room or pavilion of Durga-devi are pleasant for look as they are adorned with the sculptures of lions in lying posture, the divine goblins at the corners and the deified forms of Sakti one on each side. The inner cavity of the vasanthamandapa shines also with a good fashionable painting. The wall of mahaamandapam is laid with marble slabs. The walls and the floor of Darsana mandapam the audience hall of the temple, are polished with terrazo method of work. That which inshines all these beauties and rests behind all these as the beauty of beauties is the grace of the deity of Dugadevi installed in a most appropriate position in the sanctum sanctorum. The deity clad in red silk and worn with golden diadem is remarkably won-derfull because due to the power waves of which the entire temple system glows in lustre and is made so marvellous as what is to be inferred from its history of development.

The present is a time when the moral part of the temple rites and the temple worship is almost neglected mainly because most of the authorities concerned are uninterested in the true spirit and the true import of them and this draw back is deeply felt in the orthordox section of saivism for sometimes. At this juncture the temple stands, as if take it a challenge to fulfill the need of the time by way of putting into practice the just and proper methods of rites and worship. Unlike the average temples it has a domi-nant power over the host of priests working and a mass of saivait worshipping here and get them passively involved in an intensive performance of rites and a real and devotional worship respective-ly. The systematic and efficient administration of the executive committee headed by Pandit Miss Thangammah Appakutty and the harmoney found in the devotional services of the youths in the name of volonteer corps—Thonder sabai—are to be well attributed to the same. Thus this temple is to play its role in the upliftment of the moral standared of the populace. Such is the bare minimum demanded from the existence of a temple.

The scripture of saivism avowdly stress that any of the tiny default allowed to fall in the temple rites and the worship will have its repurcussions very badly on the public and it will readily affect the moral standared of the people. So it may not be out of place to emphasise that a temple that has no power to keep up the mark, to put in other words, if the temple is powerless to get them performed in purely a religious perspective, has nothing to do in the name of good to the public.

The temple serves the society in a number of ways. It attracts every section of the society, the poor and the rich, the learned and the unlearned, the beggar and the affluent, and the young and the old and treats them all alike. It manifest a pristine pure religious atmosphere in which a mass of saiva public finds solace forgetting their distresses both mental and physical. It gives the necessary impetus to a good number of men and women especially the youths to volunteer themselves for selfless religious services. It provides facilities not only for religious worship but religious lives. Strangely enough, even in the age of kali—notorious for unreligious character—it gets the saiva youths easily involved in the fold of religious characteristics. It contributes much to promote the art of music both vocal and instrumental by way of giving more frequent chances than that are available elsewhere, to musicians to serve this temple and honouring competent musicians occasionally with valueable gifts.

This temple generously allows a good part of its abundance to be channelled towards the propagation of Sivadharma within and without its bounds. It caters for cows breeding, orphanage, a welfare centre for destitute women, regular classes for religious knowledge and devotional music for saiva children and youths, and religious sessions for udalts. It also maintens a centre of learning (Gurukulam) meant for brahmin youths that can produce learned temple priests of good demeaner and a well provided feeding centre Annashaala within its bounds. It makes good response to calls for Dharma from outside in the name of flood relief, refugee relief educational needs and medical needs.

Of all the religious sessions held under the auspices of this temple, the red coral Jublee of the saiva siddhamta mahaasamaajam of mylapore voluntarity called to be held here was hailed supreme. This session was held continually for three days in a large scale demanding more than a lakh. It attracted a good number of eminent learned pundits and religious adepts from South India and Sri Lanka and thousands of the saivite public are benefitted by it.

Out of all the extensive special agamic rites conducted by this temple, the chandihoma, a famous sacrifice meant for Durga held in 3-5 July 1983 is plausible. This homa that employed hundreds of priests headed by Prof. Dr. K. Kailasanathan, consumed more than a cart load of smith—the sacred fire-stick, gallons of ghee, heap of cereals and other accessories, bundles of cloth and bouquets of wreaths and garlands lasted for three days in an awe striking devotional admosphere to the atmost admiration of the devotees gathered in several thousands who actually witnessed the same diery form of Durgaa illustrated in Durgaa sooktam of the Rig veda when the flames of the sacred fire rose to lick the roof of the well decorated pandal erected twelve feet high in the court yard of the temple for that purpose.

The two events just referred are meant to have contributed much to the advancement of the religious as well as cultural atmosphere of this temple.

The impact of the temple on the Saiva public seems to be very intensive. The credence the public has on this temple is admirably great. They firmly belief in the authoritativeness of this temple in healing their distresses speedily and effectively. So they wrong in flocks especially on Tuesdays and festival days and perform intensive worship and they also take strenuous efforts to make this temple full-fledged. They bring with them enough of things in cash and kinds as their offer and makes the temple treasury self sufficient. Various things and accessories needed for the performance of even the very extensive rites such as the mahaakumbhaabhisheka and the chandi homa are found heaped in the temple hall with a slight verbal notice. The expenses for the big construction works such as the chariot, the temple tank, the raaja gopuram, the hall for nuptial ceremoney 'etc' easily and effortlessly met with voluntary donations. Voluntary services from technicians of all vocation are available, here and such is the impact of the temple on the saiva public.

The propagation of sivadharma is an important factor in the curriculam work of a temple. As it may be superficially felt sivadharma does not mean the maintenance of the temple and promoting the interest of worship alone. It has a lot to be included in it such as caring for the needies, the destitutes, the orphans, the victims, the ignorants and the deseased in the society out of genune love for the soul viewing it to be manifested by Siva. The Hindu scriptures repeatedly emphasise such services rendered purely in the religions perspective form the potential part of sivadharma. The most appropriate centre to do sivadharama can be the temple alone. Because the religious perspective of viewing the soul Siva—manifested will be more proper in this centre than elsewhere. We have already noted how this temple cater for these things.

So it can be avowedly claimed that by means of all the aspects of progress this temple advances to reach the upper most limit of the ideal of a Saiva temple which is to be culminated from the history of the well flourished saiva temples of the cola period the golden age in the history of tamils. According to reliable epigraphical records it is suggested that the prominent temples of that period are not the centres of mere worship but they are the unfailing sources of social as well as spiritual excellence. Almost all the social institutions such as the schools, art calaries libraries, feeding centres and even hospitals are provided by the temples within their bounds. The temple at Thiruppathy on the venkada hill can be suggested as a living example to this even today.

That the saivism provided for sivadharma having temple the centre for it reflexes the all enveloping nature of saiva philosophy which instructs that whatever good to be done to the humanity should be had purely in a religious atmosphere and that alone would be conducive to one's realization of absolute truth which is the highest level of human goal to which saivasiddhanta stands for ever.

3

The History of the Temple

The past : The famous temple of Goddess Durgadevi is situated at Tellippallai at the 8th mile on the Jaffna-Kankesanthurai road in Jaffna Peninsula, the Northern part of Sri Lanka.

The history of this temple, except for the last three decades, is not recorded and left to be realised by guess work. However, two of the past events happened to be recorded because of the close contact of this temple with the celebrated Kandaswami temple at Maviddapuram two miles north of this temple. The one event is its consecration in 1820, which might have been the first consecration of this temple took place five years after the consecration of the Maviddapuram temple, for the first time after being demolished by the Portugese, the notorious enemies of Saivaism. The other event is the first visit of the deity of Kandaswamy of Maviddapuram in 1829, to this temple for the festival Mahaanambu that falls on the Vijaya dasami day in the Tamil month of Puraddasi equivalent to the period in between the last half of September and the first half of October.

F.N. : Vijayadasami is marked by the tenth day counted from the first New Moon day of Puraddasi. Mahaanambu, the victorious or the great arrow. Mahaan-great; Ambu-arrow. A term signifying the gracious act of divinity in destroying the demon Mahisha, the buffalow headed.

What has come be pass before 1820 and how the origination of this temple took shape is under mystery. But the tradition coming down by hear-say has something to tell us. According to the tradition the in initiative move for the origination of this temple is ascribed to a period when the Saiva devotees from Jaffna frequeated their pilgrimages to the Holy and glorious places of Siva-Sakthi worship in India and the lower limit of that period cannot however be exterior to last three hundred years. It is a well known fact that the pilgrimages of those days are made out of purely on spiritual thirst such as getting enlightenment by way of invoking the grace of deities enshrined in the ancient holy places, seeking Guru, the the spiritual teacher and wayfarer through the gracious guidance of the deities worshiped then and there, and meeting the Great for purpose of being blessed by them instantaneously and acquiring spiritual powers to Saadana. The oral traditions to be heard in Jaffna has a number of pilgrims of such category and the early history of most of the village temples in Jaffna have connection with at least one of such pilgrims and this holds good with our temple in reference. The detail is as follows : There is a habitation known as Ulokodai in the south western part of Tellippallai. The very name Ulukodai is suggestive of the fact that the habitation is gifted with the rich outcome of the tillage. So it is implied that the inhabitants of the area are of well known tiller clan known as Velaalas in Tamil. It is also to be noted that the history of Jaffna as well as several habitations of Tamils in Sri Lanka and also that of South India furnish with proofs that Velaalas being staunch Saivites initiated Saiva temples, maintained them and honoured them as their proudest possessions and it has been in vogue even before the period of Tamil Kings who are famous for these affairs and our matter in question keeps pace with the same fact.

The foremost of the rich and bountiful Velaalas of Ulukodai is one Kathirkamar named after Kathirkamam the most holiest place sanctified by Lord Muruga's being in the southern most part of Sri Lanka. Being a devotee accordingly as his name is suggestive of, he engaged himself in pilgrimages to India and more than the average pilgrims of his kind, he had an special thirst for visiting the Sakthi peedams, the seats of Sivasakti which are 64 in number to be found here and there throughout India. In the pursuits of this form of worship, once Kathirkamar visited Kaasi the Benarese and went to the famous Swapneswari peedam as his last resort. Being attracted by an eminent sage residing in worship there,

Kathirkamar has been initiated by him in the practical worship of Durgadevi in Chakra form—the mystical diagram meant for Goddess Durga. Being engaged in constant worship Kathirkamar has become fully advanced in the lines of spiritual progress. He has gained even mystical powers such as to see eye to eye Durgadevi in all her divine splendour being the object of his chakra worship. After some time, being permitted by the sage he returned home taking the chakra he worshiped so far along with a kendy both blessed by his Guru.

F.N. : Kendy : A kind of brass pot with a nozzle. It is a vessel most useful in the poojaa worship of any deity. Sometimes the deity of Sakti is ceremonially imposed on it and worshiped as the deity itself. It is observable in the Snapana Pooja preceding the Abhisheka in temples.

To Kathirkamar who returned to Ulukodai his native place every chance was so favourable as to have him engaged in pursuit of worship. So it has become imperative for him to install his chakra permanently in a convenient place and he found a Bassia-Longifolia grove fitting for his worship. He installed the chakra in a manner satisfactory to the nature of his devotion at the foot of a Bassia Longi folia tree, performed regular worship to it and rested himself there in a humble manner.

Thus Kathirkamar had a nice time in worshipping the chakra to his entire satisfaction leaving aside all other pursuit of life. Day to day his mystic energy was on the increase. Various miracles are said to have happened arounding the spot of worship. One of the most plausible miracles is the arrival of a set of cobras during the time of worship. They behaved like men of self control with-out having either the sign of threatening or sense of enmity to men or other beings in the suburb. Being attracted by the saintiliness of the cobras, devotees volunteered to offer flowers in worship to them and served them with cow's milk. Thus the place of worship attracted the surrounding habitations and became popular in a few years. The increase in the number of worshippers could have demanded some form of protection from the sun and the rain and the need would have been met with a cadjan shed to begin with.

The anxiety Kathirkamar had by himself of his successor to offer pooja to the chakra was dispelled by the deity of Durga who has become visible to him because of his maturity of love for her. Goddess Durga informed him of the arrival of a good natured brahmin from Benarese for pooja worship at the appropriate time and the same was realised and Kathirkamar had quiet, calm, peaceful and nice refuge under the holy feet of Durgadevi at the end of his life. The descendants of the said brahmin are said to have been the officiating priests of this temple till very late.

The cadjan shed temple would have probably been changed in course of time into a fortified room with walls made of mud first and a bigger room made of sand then. In these forms the temple would have remained for some decades and later when the devotees of the temple became more mindful of more solid protection of the temple deity it would have been built as an stone walled shrine room with one or two other halls in the front. It would have been after such improvement in the condition of the temple that it is consecrated in 1820 as it is noticed at the outset.

The dark period : The period that falls in between 1820 and 1953 seem to have been the dark period in the history of this temple. Because we do not have any details of events that has come to pass in the period extending to Khisteen decades all that has come to be known to us of this period is that a personage Kathiresa Udaiyar by name had managed this temple for a good number of years and his son Naganathar who also is entitled as Udaiyar and Adikar later, succeeded him as Manager.

It is assumed that the temple has been managed in this period by men in succession from a certain family which would have been headed by the said Kathirkamar and the above-named two personages are the last two links of the long chain of this succession. During this period the temple would have been maintained in the same form and condition to which it has developed at the time of its first consecration. The daily pooja worship twice or thrice a day would have been the necessary occurences. Of the nature of special poojas and festivities nothing is known in detail but from old men of the area it is said to have been heard that regular puranic recital has been celebrated here in a large scale year after year and attended by a good number of men and women.

F.N. : Puranic recital is dealt with in detail at the end of this chapter.

The other important and popular event known to have been happened in this period is the festival of Mahaanambu started in 1829 and continued up to date. But unlike in these days the splendour and dignity and glamour of this festival were marvellous in the past.

F.N. : Refer the chapter, The Goddess Durga, for the special significance of Mahaanambu of this temple.

It is remarkable that the same festival has been serving as the unbroken chain of connecting link of the eminent and ancient temple at Maviddapuram with this temple. It is known that there is an agreement signed by the authorities of both the temples in or about 1829 to ascertain this connection.

The New Era

The new era in the history of this temple sets foot with the formation of a board of trustees in 1953 to manage this temple by Naganatha Udaiyar, the then Manager of this temple.

Though the Udaiyar was well gifted and influential person and possibly he could not have any difficulty in managing the temple that had a land property of 65 lachchams, single handed, yet he was not satisfied with having the responsibility of managing this temple within his family, circle alone. Purely on the perspective of temple-development he thought of decentralizing the responsibility and paved the way for its free growth by appointing a Board of Trustees connecting ten other individuals of good stead with himself and confirmed it by means of producing a trust—by deed in 1953.

F.N. : The names of trustees can be found in a separate list.

By this time the old temple building was almost deteriorating and an immediate renaisance was badly in need. So the board on trustees framed a plan for resuscitation. The deity in the sanctum sanctorum which was installed in place of the said chakra most probably by the time of the first consecration in 1820, was ceremoniously removed to a temporary shrine room to be called Baalaalaya found in the temple premises. The extant shrine room and Mahamandapa was demolished and foundation was laid on the 6th day of Aavani 1953. The chance of laying the first stone in the foundation fell on a great man of Tellippallai, Kanagasundaram by name. The settling of the first line over the foundation has been initiated on 9.2.1954. Sir Kanthiah Vaithianathan, then Manager and the Secretary of the restoration society of Thirukketheeswaram has been blessed with getting the chance of laying the first stone and initiated the construction work known as Varikkal Naadduthal in Tamil.

The untiring efforts of the pious devotees of Durgadevi in this construction move especially that of the late Mr. Thampu-Ponnampalam who is said to have been inspired by Yoga Swami of Colombuthurai to enjoin himself vigorously, are commendable. The construction work was planned out to be made in purely strong white stones artistically fashioned. So it took its own time and a period of ten years was needed to complete the shrine room and the Mahamandapam. The financial report published by the Board of Trustee on 7.4.62 contains the details of this work.

With a view of giving more efficiency to this construction work the Board of Trustee called for a General Meeting on 5.5.62 and formed a fresh construction society in which the said Ponnampalam was proposed and seconded as secretary. C. Thiagarajah and K. Subramaniam were elected as the president and the Treasurer respectively. With this turn the Secretary began to move speedily and made arrangements for the construction of the third temple hall known as the Nirutta Mandapam equivalent to an audience hall in place and caused a new well to be found in front of the temple with the donation of Dr. Kumarapathi. He also found ways and means to get the new deities to be installed on the new temple such as Durga, Bairavar, Nagathambiran, nandi and Balipeedam, deified by Periasami a famous architect and reputed sculptor who is at that time engaged in the Maviddapuram restoration work. The new shrines for Bairava and Nagathambiran were caused to be built by Thambipillai Ponnampalam and V. Thavamani respectively. The financial report published on 31.3.64 gives all the details of these works.

The construction society was revised in order to give still more expediency and potency to the works undertaken. The revision was made on 3.5.65. As a result of this the Secretary's hand was strengthened by way of adding to him K. Sivaraja as the Assistant Secretary and Mr. Arumuganathan was elected as the new Treasurer. Tremendous progress was made in the construction work by this time which is also commended upon as the second stage of development in the new era. The following are the new aspects of progress with the respective donors :

1. The new Vinayaka shrine—Sinnadurai & Bros.
2. The seats for Nandi and Bali Peedam—S. Nagalingam
3. The fourth Hall Stampa Mandapam—Organisers of Musical Concert held in aid of the temple construction work
4. Electric Light—S. Thavamany and A. Kanagasabai
5. The Vimanamover the Sanctorum—C Thiagarajah & family.

Being attracted by these tremendous changes in the temple building the youths of the area began to play their role. They formed themselves into a volunteer corps—Thondar Sabai—and performed devotional services—Thiruppani—in the temple premises and helped up the progress of the building work not only with their manual works but also collecting public money in favour of the building expenses. It is said that they were responsible for the construction of the perimeter wall of the temple which later gave way to the development of the inner praahaara of the temple. The same volunteer corps continued to be in the temple services up to date. But some time back it was transformed as the Y.M.H.A. of Tellippallai. The Y.M.H.A. has a piece of land and a small building in it for their official purposes, near the outer gate way of the temple and by the side of the ornamental arch. It is interesting to note that the Y.M.H.A. has recentty donated a portion of land from their small holding to the development of the temple tank. The Y.M.H.A. that has become one with the temple for all purposes is solely responsible now and then to maintain perfect orderliness in the temple worship especially during the annual festivals attended by several thousands without giving room even to a slight part of discontentment felt by any of the worshipper concerned. The annual reports of the temple society never fails to commend upon the calm. quiet efficient and excellent voluntary services of the Y.M H A. which is a living example to what is the due share of the nation of youths in the upholding of the religious interest.

It is beyond need to say that the temple formation and the attendant circumstances are by now up to the mark fitting for consecration The Secretary T. Ponnampalam shouldered by himself the entire responsibility of collecting money and other accessories needed for the consecration ceremony. By virtue of the agreement made as early as 1829 which authorised the priests of Maviddapuram temple to perform the consecration of this temple, the same priets headed by Sivasiri Duraiswami Kurukkal were solicited for the consecration ceremony. Under the instruction of Duraiswami Kurukkal Sivasiri Sanmuganatha Kurukkal, the latter's eldest son and the heir to Maviddapuram temple managership took the position of the Chief Priest and performed the ceremonial rites with strenuous efforts having Mr. Ponnampalam the 'Yajamaen' one who swerves on behalf of the public to be responsible person for a temple ceremony. The extensive ceremony took three days The concluding part of the ceremony known as Kumba Abishekam—to annoint the fresh deity with the sacred divine water filled in a pot ceremonially sanctified and worshipped as the deity itself in the preceding holy rites—Yajna—was performed in the luky hora of leo on a Wednesday joined with the steller Thiruvonam of the Tamil month Aavany in the Hindu year Visvaa vasu—the giver of all wealth—by name, equivalent to 3.9 1965 This Mahakumba Abishekam which is largely attended by devotees performed by a host of Siva Achariyas and blessed by Yogis and Jnanis was proved to be the turning point of evolving Durgadevi's grace that was being involved for some time due to the absence of proper ceremonial rites the special poojas, festivals, the puranic recitals and bhajans 'etc' and with this turn the popularity of the temple began to increase in hop and while.

Then after nine months the board of trustees held a meeting on 18.5.1966 and reorganised the board by way of filling the vacancies created by members left for various causes. The new finds are S. Tarmalingam, K. Balasingham, N. Thirunavukkarasu, A. Sivapadasundram, and K. Thananayagam. At the same meeting, an executive committee consisting of 15 individuals of religious merit was appointed and given full authority in the temple management. As a result of this from June 1966 onwards the board of trustee has remained contended with being mere witnesses of the temple affairs except having the attorney power over the immoveable properties of the temple. This is to be meant as a more generous act than that Naganatha Udaiyar did early in 1953. If to say Udaiyar paved the way for the free growth of the temple it can also be said that the board of trustees cemented and polished it. However, it may need some explanation.

F.N.: Unlike the management of other institutions the temple management is characterised as Sivadharma, a kind of charitable duty of divinity which is possible only for those who can raise his inner self to the position of being Siva himself at least in his super conscious mind level, if not in real. So, it is hardly manageable for all excepting Siva Inanis the enlightened ones. In this view point those who happened to be the temple authorities should have to be ever fear striken because of their tendency to err due to their human nature. So, on the perspective of the good of the temple it is the bounden duty of the authorities concerned not to lose any chance to give up their offices whenever they get fitting men felt to be better than themselves even to a slight degree in religiousness. Such being the moral part of the issue the generous act of the Naganatha Udaiyar first and that of the board of trustees second is highly laudable. They are more sensible and more meritorious men in this world than the average ones of that category.

The Chiefs of the Executive Committee with the respective offices held by them are as follows :

C. Thiagarajah	—	The President
Nama Sivapragasam A. Subramaniam	}	The Vice Presidents
R. Rajendarm Siva Vakeesar	}	The Joint Secretary
Pundit Miss. Thangammah Appacuddy	—	The Treasurer (General)
T. Arumugaswami	—	The Treasurer for the building section.

The Committee has proved its worth by way of completing the following in a period of three years 1966—1969.

The Sthampa Mandapam	—donated by A. Kanagaratnam and family.
The Vasantha Mandapam	—donated by Attorney P. Kandiah
The Perimeter walls	—donated by Y.M.H.A. and Malaysian devotees.
The Belfy Tower	—donated by the Inhabitants of Mahathanai
The Outer Hall of the Temple	—donated by A. Kanagasabai Thambipillai Ponnampalam & others.
The Temple office	—donated by Sivanandavalli, Kanagarayar and others.
The room for the sacred fire place	—donated by Dr. S. Sinnathambi.
The Inner gate	—donated by K. Jananayakam
The Outer gate	—donated by T. Arumainayakam

All these aspects of development marked the fitness of the temple for the festival proper to be called the Brahmotsava that begins with hoisting of the temple flag and ends with the water cutting and ceremoniously observed according to prescribed rules in the

Saivagamas. Such Brahmotsava in this temple started for the first time in a day connected with the Pooram steller in the bright half of the moon—Suklapaksha—of the Tamil month Avaniy in 1968 and ended on the twelfth day and it is being conducted year after year in the same period that falls in between the days connected with Pooram and Thiruvonam both inclusive.

The Brahmotsavam in this temple is renouned for its orderliness, devotional atmosphere and the blissful contentment felt by the devotees. The kind and harmonious services of the v olunteer corps otherwise known as the Y.M.H.A. of Tellippallai forms a good part of the excellence of the features of the fes tivals. One of the special feature of this festivals is the fee ding of devotees throughout the festive season. The chariot festiv al is a land mark of the temple greatness which is attended by several thousands of worshippers rushing from almost all parts of the No rtern region of Sri Lanka.

In the period falls in between 1968 and 1974 the Executive Committee had to undergo many changes. One of the remarkable change is the appointment of Mr. T.T. Jayaratnam, the repurted Principal of Mahajana College, one of the outstanding Colleges in Sri Lanka, in place of C. Thiagarajah, who resigned his presidentship because of his illness. The other one is the election of K. Thanikasalam as joint Secretary in place of N. Kathirkamanath an who met with an untimely death. It is also to be noted that V. Selvaratnam was elected as the Treasurer (Building bran ch) in place of T. Arumugaswami, who retired due to lack of sound health.

The Board of Trustees also met with some changes in this period because some of its members died and some went abroad.

In May 1974, the Executive Committee celebrated the Silver Jubilee to mark the twenty fifth year of the well reputed elocution services of Pundit Miss. Thangamma Appacuddy who rendered valuable services to the uninterrupted restoration work of the Temple not only by her official capacity of being the Treasurer of the Executive Committee but also by her private capacity of being an excellent versatile and sweet orator in Tamil in subjects dealing with Saivaism. The soul captivating nature of her lectures acquainted Durgadevi's unimagineable greatness with the public in every nook and corner of Saiva lands including South India, Singapore, and Malaysia and caused especially the wealthy ones to contribute liberally to the construction work of this temple. The Committee in this function fittingly honoured her by awarding on her the honourary title "Durga Dhurandhari" a most significant term for so much as this lady has functioned in her official as well as private capacity of efficiently as to make others feel that she herself enshoulder the entire burden of financial implication relating the restoration work of Durgadevi temple from the very date when she proposed to be an ordinary member in the construction society.

The Golden Age : That the above noted grand and graceful event being blessed by Durgadevi has given a fresh impetus to further development of the temple is to be observed by means of the move of expediency found in temple works enlisted hereafter :

1. Vahana Shaala—The hall for accomodating the vahans—meant for vehicles to be mounted by the temple deity in festivals.
2. Thirumurai Madam—The mut meant for recital of Thirumurais, the spontaneous out pourings of devotional songs in various forms from the Saiva Saints
3. he straight path from the main road—Formerly the path leading to the temple from the main road has a curve because of an intervening piece of private land. Now, the land is acquired by the temple society and the path was made straight.
4. The widening of the outer Prahara—Formerly the outer prahara—Tet Veethy—of the temple was strait in the west and the north borders of the temple land. Now arrangements were made with the owners of the land off the borders and the outer prahara was widened by way of adding some pieces of their lands
5. Thirunandanavanam—The sacred flower garden found in the open place adjacent to the temple well, for purpose of picking flowers for poojas and decorating the deity.

6. Public Lavatory—Demanded by the increase of devotees day to day.
7. Temple Office—From 23.1.73, the system of issuing tickets for Archana is in practice This system has been brought into effect by Mr. T.T. Jayaratnam the President. The money realised in this way not only helps for the payment of the temple priests and the other employees but also meets with a considerable part of the expenses of the development work.
8. Water Resevoir—It is to be noted that the whole expenses of setting a large water reservoir and proper pipe system was met with the balance of the money being collected by Thankiasalam per year for the flag-hoisting festival.
9. Renovation of Vasanthamandapam—The Vasanta Mandapam is the hall made for the special pooja worship of the deity resting in state in all its paraphernalia even as a King in his court room or pavillion. This hall in this temple is reformed and fashioned out comparavtively in a better method and looks marvellous with excellent painting.
10. Annadaana Salaa—The apartment provided for food giving. It is a lengthy and spacious hall put up to the east of the Anaathasalaa by S. Arumuganathan. an ardent devotee of Goddess Durga.
11. Pilgrim's Resting Hall—It is put up to the most of Thirumurai Mandapam and donated by M. Ponnudurai.
12. Roofing the Inner Prahara—This sacred work planned out in 1974 and met half the way in the same year and the rest was completed in a couple of years. A considerable part of the money needed for this great work is realised by the clocution services of Pundit Miss Thangamma Appacuddy who toured for lectures in Malaysia and Singapore in the years. Those who were inspired by her lectures Volenteered to donate liberaly.
13. The Shrine of Bala Subramaniyar—This shrine found place in the North West corner of the inner Prahaara of the temple and consecrated on 18.3.76. The expenses were met with the money donated by T. Thambiraja family.
14. Gajalukshmi shrine—Gajalukshmi is the deity of Goddess

Lukshmi with two deified elephants standing on hinder legs on either side adorning the deity's head with lotus flowers holding in their trunks. The shrine found on the left hand side of the Balasubramaniyar shrine was donated by S. Balakumar. E. Kathirkamalingam and S Subramaniam are two names worth mention here for their generous act of sharing the expenses needed for the deities of Bala Subramaniyar and Gajalukshmi fashioned out in solid granite.

The demise of the President—Thiru T.T. Jayaratnam functioned as the President of the Executive Committee continually for six years. The above noted categories of developments were carried on efficiently under his close vigilance. The experience he had already gained being the able Principal of a leading College helped him to a great extent for maintaining rules and discipline in the temple service It is time that the temple society expected much from his invaluable services and pray for long life for him. But alas! His life is abruptly ended on 19.10.76. He took refuge under the holy feet of Durgadevi He will ever ramain in the fresh memory of Durgaa devotees.

The Acting President—A regular worshipper and pious devotee of Durgadevi is Thiru R.N. Sivapragasam. He has been one of the Vice Presidents of the temple society from the very inception of it and rendered valuable services to the progress of the temple by way of being a good legal adviser. He kindly consented to take up the presidentship rendered vacant by the demise of T.T. Jayaratnam and discharged his duties efficiently for some months but could not continue in it due to old age.

The New President—When the Executive Committee assembled to elect a new President in 1977, the name Pundit Miss Thangamma Appacuddy was unanimously suggested and she took office as President This gentle lady is a well known and highly appreciated figure throughout the Tamil Saiva Land as an eloquent speaker of Tamil Saivaism. She was also leading a pure live of celebacy. As we have observed it in a previous occasion her lectures in various parts of Sri Lanka, as well as India, Malaysia and Singapore earned a good name and fame for Durgadevi temple and attracted people of generosity from everywhere and this caused a number of donations to proceed towards the renovation work of the temple. It will no way become a flattery that the history of the temple of Durgadevi set foot in its golden age with this lady as the President of the temple society.

She is continuing as the President dedicating her whole live for a good efficient administration of the temple and for the propagation of Sivadharma in its premises. Her sence of dedication to the temple is marked by her untimely and sudden resignation from her former office as a well honoured teacher in a leading College at Tellippallai itself.

By the time when the new President took office the inner development of the temple work is almost over and the outer development such as the construction of a chariot with an artistic excellence, erecting a Raja Gopuram as the best of its kind and finding a temple tank fitting for the eminence and the excellence of the temple are lacking. The initiative move for the chariot construction was held in 1976 when the former President was alive and as soon as new President took office on 20.01.77 the construction work started with A. Thambithurai the reputed art inspector, as the Chief Architect of the work and the grand work of the huge and massive chariot, the best of its kind among that in average temples is finished in two years. With the completion of this chariot, the chariot festival in Durgadevi temple became to be a big pompous and elegant event. A few words to mark the special features of the chariot festival would do.

The deity of golden image finely decorated arises to the chariot with all the array of paraphernalia specially arranged as if it floats in the milky ocean of sweet musical sound aroused by a long line of Naathasuwram players and drum beaters apart from the tumultuous sound of Arohara. Thus the entire temple premises will shine in a blissful holy atmosphere of divinity in the day of the chariot festival.

Then the construction of Rajagopuram was started in an auspicious moment. For want of getting an special architect for this work, the President took a trip to Madras and contacted Thiru S. Devalingam of Valavanoor introduced by Swami Haridas the di ciple of Gnanandagiri Swamigal of Thirukovaloor. Swami Haridas who became a favourite of this temple being attracted by the amiable and devotional character ot the President helped in a number of ways towards the excellent tinish of this Rajagopuram being vigilant up to the event of its consecration held on 17.4.1987. This Raja Gopuram work was planned out in a large scale demanding more than 9 lakhs It was five tiered rising to the heigh of 63 feet with all its attributes current in tradition and finished in a couple of years without interruption due to financial implication. Swami Haridas has come all the way from Madras to its consecration held as a part of the Maha Kumba Abishekam of the temple in 1987. The Swami rested here for three days and graced the occasion in many ways. He brought with him various unguents useful for sonsecration and valuable silk - Pee'hamparams—to be presented to the priests taking pait in the ceremonial rites, and he also came accompanied with a band of good musicians on his own account and caused a good musical recital and lecture done during the days of consecration The Maha Kumba Abisheakam was devotees and it was felt as the most blessful event of all the temple ceremonies.

The other important item of the outer development of this temple was finding a temple tank worthy of the greatness of the temple. The tank. to be visited by the temple deity on the day of the festival of water-cutting ceremony was dug out in the dimension of in front of the outer gate of the temple premises. It is adorned with fire step—making on all the four sides with pure strong white stones artistically fashioned and fenced with strong iron pipes and decorated with an array of sculptural sacred pots resting on the posts standing in support of the fence. The most spacious and the most striking feature of this temple tank is praised as a novelty added to this temple view It shines also with a beautiful and well shaped fine shrine on the west edge of it which serves as the resting place of the deity visiting it in the occasion of the water-cutting ceremony. It is to be noted that the entire work was done very speedily and finished within one year and the ceremony of Theertha Prathishtaa, the ceremonial site of sanctifying if fit for the holy act of water-cutting by the deity book pl ce in August 1982.

Further in 1983 the construction of a new Subra Mancham a form of vehicle to be mounted by the temple deity on the tenth day of the festival season. It is formed entirely in iron wood (paalai). Its workmanship and the artistic beauty is praiseworthy. There are also other developments of religious character in the vicinity of the temple that are mentioned under the Section—the propagation of Sivadharma—in a separate article titled as "The Temple".

Thus the executive Committee headed by Pundit Miss. Thangaamma Appacuddy is advancing quickly in the outer development of the temple. It has a detailed scheme of things for further development. The mostly abiding and amiable character of the members of this Committee suggests that it will not fail to raise the temple premises to a township as the ancient Mathoddam of Sri Lanka and Madurai of South India, through the boundless grace of Goddess Durga. One may observe that there are various institutions coming up in the name of Durgaa in the surroundings of the temple and the particular region is begun to be called Durgaapuram.

END

The Puranic recital—It was a popular habit to recite puranas continually for a period of three months in a year at least, in the Saiva temples and it has become before long, the part and parcel of the special character of Saiva temples. The purpose of this function is to educate the mass in religious knowledge in a devotional atmosphere having the temple the most appropriate centre for it. The Saiva tradition firmly believes in that the mere worship without the fundamental knowledge in religious aspects cannot do good for humanity and that is why the importance was given to puranic recital in the Saiva temples.

The puranic recital is envisaged with certain rules and regulations of it. Both the recitors and listeners of Purana should have got at least the first step of Siva deeksha to be hold Samaya deekshaa, they should keep themselves away from the unreligious nature of daily live. They should attend the recital regularly from the beginning to the end of the Purana. They should attend to the temple pooja performed before the time of recital.

The recital is performed in a peculiar manner in which two devotees of good learning serve as the main functionaries, one to read the purana in verse and the other to explain the verse read. Both of them should sit in the temple hall the nirutta mandapam one facing northward and the other eastward. Then both of them with their hands made together in worship should sing the salutary verse of the purana meant for the invoking the grace of the deity mostly Vinayaka and the listeners also should follow suit.

Then the devotee facing northwards will read the first verse in the portion allocated for the day in a melodious voice. After reading the entire verse he repeats it again in portions. As soon as he stopped at the end of one portion the other devotee will explain it in the same melodious voice or similar voice of the former. His definition will come out in a simple language as easy as to be grasped even by a men or women of poor learning. Being so such recitals were attended by a mass of men and women in those days. The recitors will continue to three or four hours a day in the same manner as noted above and the listeners will be attending to it patiently and devotedly.

The recital their is going uninteruptedly to a prescribed period will not fail to impart a good knowledge of religious as pects. Thus the paranic recital served as the mass readia of aderet Education of the time.

The puranas entirely reveal the characteristic of Gods in general and the pre-eminence of Siva and Sakthi in special. The nature of Sakthi that works within and without of man. The miraculous aspects of divinity and the history of the sages and devotees who gained much in their secular as well as spiritual lives through their devotional and pious worship and religious austerities made in and around the temple. They give detailed accounts of the various forms of manifestations of Siva and Sakthi and the manner of worship to be paid to every one of them and the penances to be observed in honour of them.

Apart from such theological instructions the puranas also throw a beacon light on the Saiva philosophy The give categorical definitions of the three entities of Saiva philosophy and four fold path the Chariya, Kriya, Yoga and Jnana – the pure worship by way of getting the bodily limbs directly on the devotional services to God. The intensive worship by way of getting the outer and inner energy of the man directed in adoring God, a concentrated worship by way of absorbing one's inner self directly on the reality and the worship in the light of enlightenment by way of losing himself entirely and surrender himself absolutely to the grace of God and enjoying the final bless thereof respectively.

Being such the puranas are of immense value for so much as they used to impart philosophical knowledge in a simple, solemn and proper manner to the man and at the same time giving them practical training in such a manner as to produce in them the good qualities of devotion, self restraint, obedience tolerance and piecy. Thus the puranas played an important tole in the upliftment of a sense of culture as well as civilization even among the uneducated mass.

One should not need to hesitatc to suggest that the uneducated men and women regularly attended to puranic recitation in those days are not less cultured than the educated men of these days. That they are even more than these in that respect is an open secret.

Undoubtedly it was the effect of the same puranic recitals that the temple of those days are developed in pure religious atmosphere true to the sense of the word and they were gifted with an ability to guide the people not to serve from the correct path that is Sanmarga in a general sense. And it is not out of place to suggest that the rapid growth and the excellent development of our Durgadevi temple to be observed in these days is mainly due to its keeping and maintaining the rare tradition of puranic recital up to date.

The Main Entrance

The Durga (Braoze Icon)
The Festival Deity of the Temple

The Durga (Granite Stone)
The Deity in the Sanctum Sanctorum

Professor of Hindu Civilization of Jaffna University Kailasanatha Kunakhal performing the Chandi Homa in the Temple

The Mandapam at the Holy Tank Thirthakkulam

The Temple Chariot or a Car Festival Day

The Chief Guest at the Chandi Homa

The Chandi Homa at the Temple

The Holy Tample Thirthakkulan

The MADAM in the Temple court yard where regular classes and nutal held

Cow Fostering
The Go-Sala at the temple

*The Raja Gopuram of the Temple
on either side are the Shrines for Sankanithi
and Patuananuthi*